VISION

FOCUS ON WHAT MATTERS

Chris Russo

Copyright © 2019 Christopher Russo

All rights reserved. No part of this publication may be reproduced, distributed, or transmitted in any form of by any means, including photocopying, recording, or other electronic or mechanical methods, without the prior written permission of the publisher, except in the case of brief quotations embodied in critical reviews and certain other noncommercial uses permitted by copyright law.

www.officialchrisrusso.com

ISBN: 978-0-578-46871-6

First Edition

Printed in the United States of America

DEDICATION

This book is dedicated to my three amazing sons: Isaac, Jonathan, and Samuel. My deepest prayer for each of you is that you will find the vision God has for each of your lives and run hard after it. I look forward to all of the adventures we'll have together, and I'm so grateful to be your dad.

FOREWORD

A few years ago I had the opportunity to serve on a medical mission trip to Nicaragua with our church. My specific role for the trip was to run the eyeglass clinic. Although my training was limited to a few briefings on the plane ride over, my enthusiasm was high. (If you are an actual optometrist you may want to skip the foreword and jump straight to the good stuff.)

On the third day of clinic, a nurse accompanied an older woman into the clinic who was legally blind. My mission was to find a pair of glasses that could help. So, I wrote "God Loves Me" on a chalkboard and went through my routine: put a pair of glasses on her and ask her to look at the board and read the message. Repeat process until she can see the message clearly. After what seemed like a hundred pairs of glasses and still no vision, she and I were both pretty exasperated. We both felt defeated and hopeless that anything would work.

Then I remembered: there was a pair of glasses that I had set aside a couple of days earlier, because I nearly got punched by a guy when he tried them on. Not only did they have huge purple frames, but the lenses were so thick that, angled right with the sun, they could start a fire. I'll never forget the look on her face when I put those glass on her. "GOD LOVES ME! GOD LOVES ME! I CAN SEE!" It was one of the most powerful moments of my life to see her countenance immediately come alive and tears of joy stream down her face.

I can only imagine what it's like to go from barely seeing at all to seeing something crystal clear. However, I do know what it's like to go from not having vision in my life, to having clarity and purpose. Without vision, the days just seem to pass by, one after the other, slowly fading into memory. It can feel like you are sleepwalking through your life. Hopelessness and despair can feel like constant companions.

But in the moment that you see clearly, every moment has meaning and every interaction is filled with possibility.

I'm believing that the book that you are holding right now has the potential to lead you into an "I CAN SEE" moment for yourself. As you turn each page, my hope is that you begin to see a little more clearly, and that by the end of this book you find yourself jumping up and down and yelling, "I CAN SEE!"

Chris Russo is a man of vision and purpose, and he lives his life with a sense of urgency. I'm so grateful that he has opened up his life and leadership so that we can find clarity and vision as well!

Josh Surratt
Lead Pastor of Seacoast Church

INTRODUCTION

I long to live a successful life. I would bet if you didn't desire the same, you wouldn't be holding this book right now. The only question is, how do you define success? Regardless of your answer, the chances of your version of success being the exact same as the person next to you is pretty slim. This reality, that each of us carries a different version of success in our minds, has always fascinated me. When I, like so many others, long to make the most of the time I've been given, how do I make sure my life is well-spent?

One of the greatest tragedies I can think of is a wasted life. How do we make sure we don't miss the mark? How do we make sure we focus on what truly matters? How do we distance ourselves from the barrage of distractions we all encounter every day and live lives focused on things that have eternal significance?

I believe we have all been created for a purpose that far exceeds our wildest dreams. I believe the One who created us desires an intimate relationship with each of us and wants to use our gifts, talents, and stories to impact the world in ways we can't comprehend.

We are creatures who desire and thrive on inspiration. Vision has the power to focus and align our efforts like nothing else can. Vision can motivate us to run towards a better future and to push aside anything that hinders that future from coming to pass. My hope is that through these pages, you will find inspiration to seek with greater intensity what in the world you've been put on this earth to do.

Vision is a topic that's resonated with me throughout my whole life. Pastor Andy Stanley's book, *Visioneering: God's Blueprint for Developing and Maintaining Personal Vision*, defines vision as, "a clear mental picture of what could be, fueled by the conviction that it should be." Without vision, life can feel meaningless and directionless. With vision, every day can be filled with purpose and conviction. I realize the word vision can be used in many different ways. We've all had our fill of empty mantras and inspiring coffee mug quotes. Vision, like so many other powerful words, has become another junk drawer with a million different connotations stuffed into it. Real vision is a picture of the future that truly grabs you; it's something you would fight for.

As a teenager, it was the vision of various movie characters that drew me in and engaged me. Characters like Andy Dufresne from *Shawshank Redemption*, Rudy Ruettiger from *Rudy*, and (of course) Rocky Balboa from the *Rocky* series. The underdog filled with passion and a vision of victory that fueled every decision was a storyline that captured my heart in a way I couldn't explain. The passion of these characters actually captivated me so much that as a 23-year-old, I joined a boxing gym with reels of championship wins flickering in my mind. There were, of course, just a couple of challenges that I needed to address. First: it might be difficult for me to explain their pastor's black eye or broken nose to church members on Sundays. Second: boxing is really, really hard. Not having much in the way of resolving these two challenges, I gave up my boxing ambitions after only one month.

Regardless of my short-lived dreams, Rocky still inspired me. He had a vision of becoming the heavyweight champion of the world, and no person or thing would stand in his way. He faced incredible adversity, but the strength of the opposition stiffened his resolve to do whatever it took to be the best. Rocky's journey wasn't perfect (or realistic) by any means. In *Rocky III*, he let his success go to his head and that passion began to slip; he lost that "eye of the tiger."

In losing sight of his purpose, Rocky's ship wandered off course. He knew where he wanted to end up; that was never forgotten. But without intentionally making the effort to drive in that direction, to steer the ship toward his vision, his life began to flow with the familiar tide of wandering and apathy.

This simple story paints it so clearly: vision is incredibly powerful. Vision creates significant friction with the status quo of today because the picture of the future it presents has not yet become a reality. Take that in one more time. Vision creates friction with today, because its picture of the future has not yet become reality. It isn't comfortable, easy, or for the faint of heart. It requires change. It creates challenge. Once a compelling picture of the future grips you, it becomes a part of who you are, and you can't shake it. You can try to forget about it or run from it, but that picture lingers in your soul. It reminds you that there is a life out there that utilizes everything God made you to be. It invites you to stand up and keep going. I'm looking forward to this journey together.

CONTENTS

	FOREWORD	v
	INTRODUCTION	vii
Chapter 1	FINDING DIRECTION	1
Chapter 2	MISSING THE TARGET	5
Chapter 3	FINDING WHAT MATTERS	7
Chapter 4	BEGINNING A JOURNEY	11
Chapter 5	WRITING IT DOWN	15
Chapter 6	ENGAGING OUR ENEMY	23
Chapter 7	WITH OPEN EYES	27
Chapter 8	TAKING ANOTHER STEP	33
Chapter 9	EMBRACING THE JOURNEY	37
Chapter 10	LINKING ARMS	41
Chapter 11	ORDINARY EFFORTS, EXTRAORDINARY POWER	45
Chapter 12	THROUGH A WIDER LENS	49
	A FINAL THOUGHT	51
	ACKNOWLEDGEMENTS	53
	FROM THE AUTHOR	54

1
FINDING DIRECTION

In Proverbs 29:18 (NASB), it says, "where there is no vision, the people are unrestrained." Unrestrained. It means that without vision, people simply do whatever they want without thinking ahead. Isn't that a picture of how many of us live our lives? Without vision, it doesn't really matter how we spend our money or time. That's because there's no clear, compelling picture of the future that's driving us onward. Pastor Craig Groeschel differentiates the words, "spending" and "investing." Investing has the connotation of intentionality and purpose, but spending has the connotation of flippancy and carelessness.

Vision can lead us to *invest* our time, energy, and resources instead of simply using them up with little thought. Imagine that your time on earth, your efforts, your energy, your every interaction with loved ones, coworkers, strangers, and all others are literal dollars in your hand. How are they being used? Are they being invested with purpose and planning? Are they being spent mindlessly, leaving you empty-handed and wondering where they went?

God has given you gifts and talents you may not even realize you've been blessed with. Living with vision can capture those blessings and apply them with purpose to your action and efforts. It can help you make the most of what you have to offer. Without it, you'll just drift, and nobody drifts in the right direction. Now here's the question you've been waiting for: **Do you have a vision for your life?**

My guess is that there are two general types of people who have picked up this book. The first person is one who has a clear vision in mind, but hasn't figured out exactly what to *do* with it. You may feel compelled, inspired, or driven by the vision you have, but the fear that it won't be realized is really what's keeping you up at night. How will this vision become a reality? The second person is one who is compelled or inspired by *the idea* of a vision, yet that spot remains an open blank in your heart. Your fear is in actually asking the questions that you feel inside: does God even have a vision for me? What if I'm missing it or what if I just don't figure out what God is saying?

I realize this can be an overwhelming topic to approach, but the key is this: start small and begin to ask important questions. What would constitute a vision for you? When you think about the future, where does your mind tend to go? If that future didn't happen, would it somehow make life less worth living? Is there a certain number in the bank account you aspire to? Is it a position at work? Is it a picture of what you want your family to look like? These questions are clues that can help you identify the vision you currently have.

Around the time I was twelve, my friend and his dad took me out to play my first round of golf, and I knew immediately that I was in love. I, of course, played terribly, but that didn't matter. Here was something that took focus and perseverance and dedication and that felt personal—me against all the other opponents—and I couldn't get enough. My mom passed away when I was a kid, and my teenage years were characterized by insecurity and rejection.

My mom's death felt like it removed the gravity from my life. Her presence had kept me feeling grounded and secure, and when she passed away, I lost my sense of bearing. I slowly but surely started to lose my way. A hole started to grow in my soul and with each passing year, that hole grew larger and larger. Golf seemed like my way to fix all of that, and I set my heart on it: this was my plan for the future to achieve the success that I thought would permanently satisfy the void in my life. The thought of someday playing on the PGA tour became my obsession.

I practiced in the backyard and envisioned myself competing head to head with stars like Tiger Woods and Mark O'Meara. I loved the internal nature of the sport and the focus it demanded. In golf, there isn't anyone or anything that can stand in your way, except you. If I could conquer my inner demons, practice hard, and want it bad enough, I thought I could achieve everything I wanted.

Golf was my vision. When we develop a vision for the future, a picture of what could be that's fueled by the conviction that it should be, it's tied to our deepest values, fears, and aspirations.

Our personal vision can tell us a lot about ourselves.

I thought being a professional golfer would solve all that was wrong in life. As an adult, I've come to see a few things about my PGA dreams that my teenage self didn't see. What I see now is that my golf pursuit was never really about the game of golf. It was about all that I thought golf could bring me: affirmation and acceptance and a sense of security.

I can easily see now that I wasn't meant to wear that green championship jacket, but that vision was a powerful driving force for me in those years. It drove me to practice hard and to say "no" to a lot of things, so that I could say "yes" to my dream, instead. It also taught me that hard work was a necessary part of achievement. It showed me that for anything worthwhile, victory isn't won overnight or without a fight. If you've ever chased a vision and faced the disappointment of when it fell flat, don't be discouraged.

Romans 8:28 (NIV) says, "and we know that in all things God works for the good of those who love him, who have been called according to his purpose." This means that if you'll decide to pursue Christ and all he has for you, none of the experiences in your life—whether that means a broken dream or a grieving heart—will be wasted. They haven't been for me and they won't be for you, either. God is the master of using broken pieces to pave the path toward purpose.

2
MISSING THE TARGET

In the 2004 Olympic games in Athens, Greece, a sharp-shooter named Matt Emmons had his second gold medal all but draped around his neck, or so he thought. In the 50-meter three-position rifle final, Emmons only needed a shot near the bullseye to take home that medal. Emmons fired his shot, and he was certain it was good, but the target didn't register it. Emmons looked to the officials for reassurance. It's rare, but sometimes the electronic targets do fail. What could possibly be the reason his shot hadn't registered?

It turns out, he'd fired a perfect shot, only the mark had been made on the wrong target. Emmons had accidentally fired at the target in the adjacent lane, missing his own target completely. This forced the officials to award him a score of zero, which meant finishing in 8th place. Oh, and no gold medal. I can only imagine the kind of regret, pain, and disappointment that came over him through that experience.

If Emmons felt immense heartbreak over missing the right target in the Olympics, how much more heartache do we have in store for us if we hit the wrong target in life? If we develop and fight with our lives on-the-line for a vision that's not in-line with God's purpose for us, Emmons' story could easily become our own.

Imagine the tragedy and regret that comes with getting to the end of your life and realizing you hit the wrong target. Take a minute and imagine yourself ten, twenty, or thirty years down the road of your life. What do you want to have accomplished? What does your marriage look like? How about your relationship with your kids, what's it like? What brings you joy at that phase of your life? Now think about these same areas of your life, today. If your life travels the exact same course it's currently on, will you reach that picture you envisioned? Would it be close? It may be a bit hard to acknowledge in this moment, but are there significant gaps?

One thing I want to acknowledge here is many of us have had things happen to us that we had little to no control over. I realize that most of us are not coming out of an ideal past as we try to envision what our future with God could look like. If that describes you, please don't be discouraged. God is more powerful and loving than words can describe and he can accomplish incredible feats with broken and fragmented lives. That is the story of the gospel and when you boil it down, that's the story of every person who follows Christ.

That being said, putting words to the gaps you see will help you clarify how you define success in life, and perhaps, help you begin to redefine it. My hope and prayer is that it will help you cultivate and create a vision for your life that's in-line with how the God of the universe created you.

Popular culture tells us that life is all about us, and that's how it *should* be. It tells us it's all about how much money we make, how much power we accumulate, and how big our houses are. Some might belittle those materialistic motives, but the thought of a damaged image at work, among your friends, or on social media would be devastating for you. In fact, I'd say that culture actually reflects the natural drift of every person on the planet: **to pursue our own gain.** Achieving the picture of your future self that you just envisioned won't happen by accident. The forces of culture and our own selfish drives can easily pull us off track. That means that the starting point for defining success has to be bigger than ourselves.

3
FINDING WHAT MATTERS

Our quest for vision in life can go no further unless we begin with God. God is at the center of the universe. He's not only the One who created the cosmos and all of mankind, he's the One that desires a personal, intimate relationship with each one of us. As our Creator, his ultimate plan for all of us begins with what Jesus spells out in Mark 12:30-31 (NIV): "'Love the Lord your God with all your heart and with all your soul and with all your mind and with all your strength.' The second is this: 'Love your neighbor as yourself.'" There is no commandment greater than these." When it comes to the big picture, this is what life is all about; loving God and loving others. We, as people, tend to overcomplicate things, but this is the core of our Creator's intent for us.

My first vision in life was really just about me and the affirmation, acceptance, and security I thought would come with golf stardom. God obviously had something very different for me in mind, and during my freshman year of college, He pointed me in a new direction. I started off that year doing what many new college students do. I wasn't the coolest kid in high school; I was a little too awkward to gain the attention of the girls I liked. I also wasn't the best student since clearly I was focused on other things. Once I got to college however, things started to turn around in those areas. I made some new friends, started making good grades, and managed to get the attention I'd been seeking from girls. I thought things were finally starting to work out pretty well for me, but I couldn't shake the feeling that something deep in my soul was still missing. There was a pervasive sense of emptiness that no amount of partying could seem to remedy.

Something was starting to shift in my soul. I found myself more thirsty for God, but that was something I felt more emotionally than understood intellectually. I just wanted more than the world around me had to offer. My first real prayer to God was around that time. When I was growing up, I might have prayed that I'd sink a putt on the golf course or win a baseball game, but this time, I was serious and desperate. I prayed that if there was anyone out there who could hear and help me, I was ready for it. It was like I was stranded on a deserted island with one flare left in the gun. With all the hope I could muster, I fired it up into the night sky hoping someone would see it. As I would soon find out, my prayer had been heard.

One of my new friends that year was a little different than the rest. Ashwin was my roommate, and he was very different from most of the people I'd known back in my hometown in Connecticut. He had a joy and presence about him I didn't really understand, but it was very compelling. He was cool, but he didn't do all the things typical college students do to find fulfillment and satisfaction.

Because of these different factors, Ashwin intrigued me. He had a faith in Jesus and while I couldn't articulate it at the time, the fullness he seemed to feel inside was exactly what I lacked. At one point, he actually told me that he knew he was going to heaven. His certainty just stunned me. I'd never heard someone say they were certain there *was* a heaven, let alone that they knew they were going there. He said it as matter-of-factly as if he'd said he was going to New York for the holidays. Moments like that one sparked my curiosity and left me wondering if maybe there was more to God than I really knew.

Not too long after that brief, honest prayer, I had an experience that changed everything for me. All set to return home the next day for my Christmas break, I had planned to go to a party with some friends, but I was feeling tired and decided to stay home instead. I crawled into bed, thinking I'd get a good night's rest before flying home, but a supernatural dream came over me that forever changed my life.

In the dream, I was in this dark soul and I was descending into a dark chasm. In front of me was a brilliant, shining light, and rising into it there were bright faces, including one I recognized: Ashwin. I awoke from the dream, and the meaning of the dream could not have been more clear to me; if I died at that moment, I was not going to heaven. I went directly into Ashwin's room to share what I had seen in the dream. He asked me if I wanted to pray with him, and that was the night I surrendered my life to Jesus Christ. I asked that God would come into my heart and make me the man He wanted me to be.

I immediately felt a weight lift off of my shoulders, a presence of joy came over me like I'd never felt before. It was a holy moment; the most important moment of my life, actually. Ashwin offered to let me read his Bible, and I was amazed by the power I experienced as I read it. I felt like I was reading a book from another realm, from a time beyond my own. The experience felt like something out of a fairy tale where a kid sneaks into the forbidden section of a library and picks up a book he has no business reading. To his surprise and terror, he finds the book is actually talking about him. That's how reading the Bible felt to me that night. I was amazed and knew that something life-altering had just happened to me. I woke up the next morning and knew I was truly a different person. I simultaneously knew a great journey had begun, and that I didn't have a clue what it was going to look like.

If we are going to receive vision from God for our lives, we have to start with a significant perspective shift. For me that looked like a life-altering dream; I would imagine that God will have an easier time getting your attention than he did for me. Regardless of how this perspective shift occurs, our focus needs to gradually lift from ourselves and settle onto God. To begin to focus on him, understanding what Jesus did for us is absolutely paramount. God created us to live in a loving relationship with him, but sin entered the picture and fractured our connection with God. He could have justifiably let people persist in their arrogance and rebellion, but instead, he initiated a rescue mission. Because of his unfathomable love for us, God sent his Son, Jesus Christ, into the world to live a sinless life and pay the penalty for our sins on the cross. He rose from the dead three days later and in doing so, permanently achieved eternal salvation for all who would believe in him. And even more important than understanding what he did, we must *receive* this gift of salvation for which he paid such a high price. Because of Jesus, anyone can come to God through faith in Christ and receive the complete forgiveness of their sins. Nothing we can do can earn our entrance into heaven; our sin is too great and God is too holy to allow sin into his presence. When we accept this truth, this gift of salvation, we begin a journey that will focus our lives and our future on something, *someone*, so much greater than ourselves.

4
BEGINNING A JOURNEY

Contrary to popular belief, focusing our lives on God is inextricably linked to us discovering our purpose and vision for our lives. The simple reason for this is we are created beings. Created beings simply cannot find their purpose or design apart from a relationship with their Creator. It's just impossible. When we get this essential focus backwards, the world around us and even our own life becomes distorted. Imagine yourself on a bright, clear morning on wide-open mountainous land. You've decided to get a closer look at the scenery and wildlife using a telescope. Except the only problem is you're looking through it backwards. The world through that lens becomes small and insignificant, and the only thing magnified is you.

Tragically, this is how many people live their lives. Their focus centers around themselves. They see God and other people as being insignificant and distant, but their needs, their desires, their dreams far outweigh everything else. God and other people are merely supporting actors and actresses in a drama starring you-know-who. Life is not meant to be lived this way, but it's the intended or unintended path that many have chosen. The perfect example of the human predisposition to focus on ourselves is the pure and honest selfish nature of a three-year-old. I happen to have a three-year-old of my own, and while our little Sammy is a treasure and a joy, he's no exception to this rule. This is where we all start in life, but it's not where we're supposed to end up. The hope is that as we mature, our attention will gradually shift from simply meeting our own needs and fulfilling our own desires to pursuing God's desires and meeting the needs of others.

If we engage in the process of growth and maturation, we begin to learn that we are actually not the stars of the drama. This story speaks of a holy and powerful God, and we get to participate in pointing to His glory. We can worship him and cultivate a relationship with him through the Bible and prayer. As that relationship continues to grow, something else happens. That telescope begins to turn around, and God's work in others' lives comes into focus. We start to see that we are here to be used by God in the service of others.

For a moment, think of the people in your life. When you see your neighbor, do you see someone you wished would do a better job cutting his grass? What about your coworkers? Are they competitors who have received opportunities that could have been yours? What about the family member who seems to always make things complicated? What if you knew what was in their heart, what if you knew how God intends to use them? What if you could see the story that God was writing through each of them? When the telescope is focused in the right direction, we stop seeing others in a coldly distant, judgmental way, and we begin to see them as being created in the image of God. We become interested in their stories and in partnering with God for their ultimate restoration.

It's important to remember though, that shifting our perspective, that turning the telescope in the right direction, is not a one-time thing. When I was young, the vision I had for my life was all about my own glory and popularity. But even now, it's easy for my focus to drift back to my own gain. It takes intentional daily decisions to refocus my soul in the right place, day after day, year after year. For me personally, I spend regular time in God's word, prayer, and around people who challenge me to focus on what really matters. This is part of how I pursue turning the telescope around. What would turning the telescope around look like in your life? If we're going to get a vision for our lives that matters, we have to start with God. We must live our lives focused on him. Trying to get a vision for your life from God without centering your life on Him is essentially asking Him to be your divine administrative assistant. It's asking Him to give you a plan or a purpose to help you fulfill your own dreams and ambitions. If that's your fundamental prayer and heart posture, frustration will follow. God has a life-altering, world-changing vision for your life, but that will only be realized as you accept the paramount reality that this life is about bringing glory to God and not to yourself. God is the author of the universe and while he did give you free will, your life only grows if you choose to willingly love and worship your Creator.

If your heart resonates with the need to shift your perspective onto God, whether this is the first time or thousandth time, you can follow this short prayer as a guide:

> *God, I recognize life is not about me. I repent of all the ways I've tried to control my own life and destiny. Lord, from here on out, I want my life to be focused on you. Help me surrender all I am and all I have to you. Use me however you want to every single day of my life. Help me to see how you're using me in the lives of those around me. I pray that I would be a reflection of your love to them and to the world. Empty me of myself and help me to trust you with all my heart and soul. In Jesus' name, Amen.*

5
WRITING IT DOWN

Go back and reread that last prayer one more time. Read it slowly and let it sink in for a breath before continuing. As we turn the telescope around and life becomes focused more on God than on ourselves, we move into a position that allows us to receive more of God's vision for our lives.

As we become students of God's word, cultivate a growing prayer life, and surround ourselves with others who are doing the same, we will gradually begin to understand God's heart for us and for the world around us.

In Jeremiah 29:13 (NIV), God says, "You will seek me and find me when you seek me with all your heart." This verse shows us a couple of things about the way life works. One: God wants to be found by us and he wants to reveal himself to us. Two: engagement in this journey calls for an all-in pursuit and not just a lukewarm, intellectual acknowledgement of certain beliefs. If we begin to set our hearts and minds on seeking and pursuing the heart of God, he is going to begin wiring into us his plans and purposes for our lives.

It's not the act of writing your vision down that gives it power. It is the act of giving yourself a few concentrated moments to focus on the words that describe the thoughts in your mind and heart that gives vision power. It's all too easy to just let the days and months pass by without ever taking the time to stop and reflect on where your life is headed. Give yourself permission to take those needed few moments to pray, focus your thoughts, remove the noise from your mind, and picture where life is taking you. Take just a little time to have a prayerful moment to evaluate your life with God and ask Him if you're on the right track. Remember, our lives are finite and our time will be invested or spent in one direction or another. We get to make the choice daily as to whether we'll someday know we've taken an aimed shot at the right target or if we'll have to suffer the heartache of having spent our lives on goals and objectives that have no eternal value.

If you and I were to sit down for coffee and you were to ask me about God's vision for my life, there are certain things I would point to; they aren't achievements I've accomplished, but they constitute the direction that I aim for. In the spirit of transparency, I'd like to give you a window into my heart, and share some of the vision I believe God has given me. I know that for many people, the first step is the most difficult, so let's take that step together. My hope is that you'll read these points and see them as a jumping-off point as you begin to put your own vision into writing.

1. I will walk closely with God all of my life.

I don't believe Jesus died just so we could pray a little and perhaps read the Bible every once in a while. I don't believe he was raised to life just so we can be somewhat nicer people, or have a few good principles to help steer our day-to-day decisions. I think the purpose of his death and resurrection is much bigger than that. I believe Jesus died and rose again so we could live in a close relationship with our Creator, and I want to experience that relationship in all its fullness. I want to know the intimacy with God that Christ graciously made available to us. This picture is truly the center of life for me, and any other vision God gives me stems from this one.

2. I will love my wife with a Christ-like love every single day.

I believe, based on God's word, that marriage was created to be a picture of the love God has for his people, and that it looks like two people mutually submitting their lives to God and to one another. In so doing, they are also displaying the love of God to the world around them. Abbi and I have been married for twelve years, and every day has been a process of growth. At times, the growth has been painful and difficult. At others, it's been exciting and joyful. Either way, our goal has been to grow closer to God and one another, year after year, and I want our marriage to reflect this picture. It seems that simply staying married is what so many aspire to, but I believe there's so much more possible when two people are submitted to God and intentional about the future. That's exactly what I want to experience in my own marriage, and more.

3. I will raise my boys to be the men God created them to be, and cultivate our relationship, so that one day, they'll be my closest friends.

Now, I know I can't control the choices my boys make later on in life. They're eight, seven, and three as I write this, and they each have a lifetime of choices still to make. By God's grace though, I believe this vision is possible. I love having boys, and I love that the older they get, the more we'll be able to do together. I envision us hunting, fishing, and adventuring together. When they're adults, I want that kind of friendship with them, and I'll do everything I can to raise them in ways that will allow our relationship to grow into that one day.

4. I will invest significantly in a handful of friendships.

It's easy for me to spread myself too thin when it comes to friendships. I'm generally a social person, and I love making connections with new people in all different walks of life. The older I get though, I have begun to realize the finite nature of my capacity for friendships. I can't be friends with everyone, as much as I might want to. If I'm not careful, I could end up with tons of acquaintances but no true friends. I don't want that to be my story. I want to significantly invest my time, resources, and energy into a handful of friendships. I believe those investments will result in not just friendships, but a brotherhood, that is authentic, enduring, challenging, and supportive. In the same way that God is relational to his very core, we are relational beings. We cannot fulfill our God-given potential or walk in the abundant life of Christ without close relationships. These relationships, like anything else worth pursuing, won't happen by accident. In every season of life, I want to make sure I prioritize the cultivation of deep friendships. To not do so would be to miss a significant aspect of God's calling on my life.

5. I will voice the hope of Jesus to a hurting world.

My life was nothing before Christ. I was an angry person with very little hope and many broken and selfish ambitions. Jesus changed everything and I mean, absolutely everything. I know there are still tons of people in the world who don't know the hope I know. I realize everyone has a different faith journey and I want to respect that, but I can't water down the fact that I believe Jesus is the answer to this world's fractures and wounds. The desire to fulfill this vision in my life has led me to pastor, teach, write, and share as often as I'm given the opportunity that there is hope for you in Jesus. Turning to him can be as close and simple as whispering a desperate prayer to him, and I believe it's the most important decision each and every person can make.

These are a few snapshots of the vision I believe God has provided for my life. This list isn't exhaustive, but these are real dreams and desires I believe God has placed on my heart to see fulfilled during my short time on this earth.

So, what about you? When you think about your life and the things that matter most to you, what areas of your life do you want to have vision around?

I've included some space to begin writing down the vision God is stirring, or beginning to stir, within you. I would encourage you to start by praying and asking God to give you direction for this exercise.

Here is a prayer that might help you get started:

> *God, I ask that you would give me a picture of your vision for my life. Fill me with your Spirit and show me what's important to your heart. I offer to you my gifts, talents, abilities, and even my many shortcomings; use me however you see fit. God, all I have comes from you, and I humbly offer it all back to you. God, guide me now as I try to discern how you'd like to use me in the future. In Jesus' name, amen.*

I've provided some questions as prompts to help you find some clarity in your thoughts. I encourage to give yourself some time; you may need fifteen minutes or you may need an hour. Try to not get too focused on the practical side, but simply write down everything in your head as you consider these questions. You have plenty of time to figure out the practicalities later. Right now, the most important thing is to simply write it all down.

1. What moments or parts of your life might God want to use to impact others?
2. What unique gifts and passions do you have? How might God want to use them to impact the world around you?
3. What, if it didn't happen in your life, would cause you great regret and remorse?
4. Who has God strategically placed in your life to help you carry out the vision he's given you? How can you further cultivate those relationships?

VISION

Writing down the vision for your life isn't an exercise for you to do one time and then move on. This is something I would encourage you to practice again and again. Take this moment to put a reminder on your calendar, phone, refrigerator, or whatever works for you. Create a reminder six weeks from now to look back and re-read the notes you've recorded here. How many books have you read that impacted you enough to make you want to come back and revisit the words? I feel that way with almost every book I read. And how often have you actually gone back and done it?

For me, it's almost never. I think it's safe to assume that I'm not alone in that boat. Our lives move quickly, the distractions are endless, and on we move to the next thing. Revisiting this vision exercise in six weeks and re-reading what you wrote may stir a couple of realizations in you. One, you may be reminded of the significance of the words you wrote down. Two, you'll realize forty more days of your life have gone by and if you've moved the needle in any of the areas that matter most to you.

If at that point you feel like God leads you in a different direction than what you've already written down, simply add to your notes. The point is to continue prayerfully considering how God may want to use you and to write down whatever he gives you in the way of vision for your future.

6
ENGAGING OUR ENEMY

One of the things I've found to be true in life is that every victory comes with a fight. Whether it's graduating from college or getting your kids to school on time, there are challenges that will have to be overcome. The most worthy accomplishments can be some of the most difficult fights of your life, and following Christ is certainly no exception. It's not that God desires you to follow Him so that he can make things more difficult for you; God has good plans for you.

The journey of following God is difficult because there's an enemy who would love to see you discouraged, and that just might be the least of it. In 1st Peter 5:8 (NIV) it says, "Be alert and of sober mind. Your enemy the devil prowls around like a roaring lion looking for someone to devour." In John 10:10 (NIV) it says, "The thief comes only to steal and kill and destroy; I have come that they may have life, and have it to the full." God's vision for you involves you experiencing "life to the full," but our enemy, the devil, is looking to devour, steal, kill, or destroy anything good in your life.

You recognizing that God is the center of your story, pursuing him for vision to positively impact those around you, and getting serious about putting that vision into action means the enemy will want to stop it. Or distract you. Or discourage you, or derail you, or simply to destroy your life. Pursuing the vision God has given you means taking a step into the battle, understanding the enemy will come against that vision.

In Ephesians 6:12 (NIV), Paul teaches us, "For our struggle is not against flesh and blood, but against the rulers, against the authorities, against the powers of this dark world and against the spiritual forces of evil in the heavenly realms." So what are we struggling against, exactly?

As I mentioned before, there is a natural bent inside each of us that pulls us toward pursuing our own gain; this is the sinful nature at work in us. It creates distance from God and others, making ourselves the center of the universe. The sinful nature exists in every person, whether you've already surrendered your life to Jesus or not.

Remember the telescope turned backwards? Our sinful nature is a powerful force that pulls us into selfishness and threatens to shift our focus away from the path we desire to follow. This backwards perspective can take the form of seeking selfish gain, or the form of self-deprecating talk and behavior. Regardless of the tendency, the sinful nature will always make efforts to put the focus on self, in place of God and others.

The culture that surrounds us can also stand in the way of following a vision that God has given us. It applauds and echoes what we hear from our own sinful nature: that this life is all there is and it should only be about us. Seeking instant gratification and getting ahead at all costs are some of the subtle yet deceptive messages that our culture cheers on. In James 4:4 (NLT), it says, "You adulterers! Don't you realize that friendship with the world makes you an enemy of God? I say it again: If you want to be a friend of the world, you make yourself an enemy of God." Friendship with the culture of the world means receiving and accepting the values that the world holds in high regard, values that are based on a legacy of resisting God.

While our sinful nature and our culture can be major distractions that pull us away from a vision for our future, the devil is still our greatest enemy. He is endless in his forms of deception, and his primary objective is to sever our relationship with God and snuff out our love for others. The best understanding of the enemy I've gained was from reading *The Screwtape Letters* by C.S. Lewis. It gives a soul-stirring picture of spiritual warfare that will challenge you. It helps illustrate what the apostle Paul may have meant when he said that "Satan himself masquerades as an angel of light (2 Corinthians 11:14 NIV)". And as he longs to "steal and kill and destroy," he'll use any means necessary to deceive and distract you with the goal of your ultimate destruction.

The enemy's distractions come in so many forms it's difficult to label them. Often his distractions or attacks come through areas where we are overly sensitive or easily offended.

Are there people in your life that you feel are impossible to forgive? Or people or situations that offend you over and over, even after you thought you'd "gotten over" that issue?

Sometimes relationships that are extremely difficult may be pointing to a wound in your heart that the enemy is using against you. Pay attention to the white noise you hear in your mind throughout the day. Are there any familiar messages you find on repeat that seem to hold you back from experiencing freedom?

The most important thing to understand about the nature of spiritual warfare is that it's a battle of lies versus truth. As Jesus taught about the Devil, he said, "When he lies, he speaks his native language, for he is a liar and the father of lies (John 8:44 NIV)." What this tells me is that we need to lean into the truth heavily if we are going to live and walk victoriously in this life.

Jesus himself was attacked by the enemy before he started his public ministry. (Matthew 4:1-11 NIV) In this account, the Devil approached him three different times with three different attempts to get him to disobey his heavenly Father. You can read the story and see that Satan's attacks were very subtle and extremely deceptive, especially when you take into account that Jesus was most likely very hungry and tired after fasting forty days and forty nights.

Each time, Jesus responded to the attack by quoting the word of God back to the Devil in such a way that he was able to stomp out the temptation. In so doing, Jesus gave us an example of what it looks like to do battle with the enemy and win. We can be men and women who fight for and understand the truth of God's word. We can't afford to just have a casual relationship with our Bible; it is our lifeblood.

7
WITH OPEN EYES

Even with understanding the nature of our enemy, it still doesn't come naturally for most of us to think of ourselves as being in a spiritual battle. In fact, it's something we will need to be reminded of again and again for it to stay present in our minds. There was one year before my wife and I were married that she gave me a sword for Christmas. An actual, full-sized sword.

To be honest, I was pretty baffled at first because this wasn't something I desperately wanted or had ever even considered owning. She was clearly very excited about giving it to me though, which was even more confusing. But as she explained her reasons behind the gift, I began to understand. She wanted me to have a powerful, physical reminder that "the Word of God is living and active, sharper than any two-edged sword" (Hebrews 4:12 ESV), and that God had gifted me as a leader, and the Word of God is the sword that I would use to lead an "army." That sword hangs in my office now, and is a gift that I'll treasure forever. I'm reminded that we are actively engaged in a battle for the things that are important to us, and I don't ever want to forget that.

As you encounter the enemy, or opposition from culture and from your own sinful nature, along the road of your own God-inspired vision, remember that you also have a sword that you will lead and fight with;

that sword is the Word of God.

In a battle, the best way to achieve victory is by taking a proactive strategy. This spiritual battle is no different. Two of our most powerful offensive weapons are God's Word and prayer. One of the most clear and powerful passages of scripture written on the topic of spiritual warfare comes from the book of Ephesians. In chapter 6:10-20 (NIV), Paul said:

> *Finally, be strong in the Lord and in his mighty power. Put on the full armor of God, so that you can take your stand against the devil's schemes. For our struggle is not against flesh and blood, but against the rulers, against the authorities, against the powers of this dark world and against the spiritual forces of evil in the heavenly realms. Therefore put on the full armor of God, so that when the day of evil comes, you may be able to stand your ground, and after you have done everything, to stand. Stand firm then, with the belt of truth buckled around your waist, with the breastplate of righteousness in place, and with your feet fitted with the readiness that comes from the gospel of peace. In addition to all this, take up the shield of faith, with which you can extinguish all the flaming arrows of the evil one. Take the helmet of salvation and the sword of the Spirit, which is the word of God. And pray in the Spirit on all occasions with all kinds of prayers and requests. With this in mind, be alert and always keep on praying for all the Lord's people. Pray also for me, that whenever I speak, words may be given me so that I will fearlessly make known the mystery of the gospel, for which I am an ambassador in chains. Pray that I may declare it fearlessly, as I should.*

From my observations and experiences as a pastor, many of the Christians filling the church often take a battle stance that looks more like an army charging the beach of Normandy with beach chairs and sunscreen than it looks like courageous soldiers. So, how do we use the word of God and prayer to do battle with the enemy? Just like with many things, the best way to get better at this is by simply getting started. The Bible is a compilation of sixty-six books that were mostly written over two thousand years ago by various authors under the inspiration and guidance of the Holy Spirit. This is why the Bible can seem very intimidating or overwhelming, but that's exactly why it's so important to read the Bible in a translation you connect with and understand. Even if you start with reading for just five or ten minutes every day, it's a start.

Mornings are my best time of day, so that's when I prefer to spend time reading the Bible and in prayer, but the time of day is not something to stress about. Simply pick a time when you know you can truly focus and give your undivided attention. Regardless of your personal preferences for this concentrated time in God's word and prayer, the basics are fairly simple and straightforward.

When you begin your time with God, start with a word of prayer that he would help you to engage with the passages you're about to read. If the Bible is relatively unfamiliar to you or you struggle with what exactly to read, consider beginning with the book of Psalms and the gospel of John. The book of Psalms is essentially the Bible's prayer book, and it's full of heartfelt prayers that are sometimes gritty and reflect the full range of human emotions. The gospel of John is in the New Testament, and it focuses heavily on the love of God. It will grow your understanding of God's heart for both the entire world and for you.

Then, when you spend time reading the Bible, focus on quality over quantity. After you read the section of scripture you've chosen for the day, record your questions and observations in a journal or a notepad. Perhaps there's an insight in one of the passages that gives direct application to your life. If that's the case, write down whatever that application is and commit to taking a step of obedience to God that same day. If there's no obvious direct application, the best idea may be just highlighting whatever it is that sticks out to you and returning back to that section in the future for further reflection.

The Bible is not a book merely to be studied and comprehended intellectually. It's a book that's meant to be lived. It's deep with life-changing truths that will transform your life when read in the context of a relationship with the God who inspired it.

Incorporating prayer before, during, and after you read the Bible in your focused time with God will help you process the truths that fill its pages. Praying before you read can set your mind at ease as you talk to God about the distractions that may hinder your focus. If you come across something in your reading that disturbs you or feels difficult to understand, pause and take it to God in prayer. He is not afraid of our doubts or our difficult questions. After you're done reading and recording your observations, questions, and applications, spend some time writing down your prayers.

My guidance on prayer is plain and simple: be real. You'll find no place else where this value is demonstrated more clearly than in the book of Psalms. You won't find cookie-cutter recitations of rote religious truths there. What you will read are heartfelt cries, pleas, and praises to a living God who the authors believe can intervene and change their circumstances. That's one of my favorite things about prayer; we don't need to pretend when we pray.

We're talking to a God who understands everything about us before a word is even on our tongue, so what's the point in pretending? Whether you're angry, scared, jealous, tired, or whatever else, start where you are. Even if you're struggling to believe God exists, start exactly there. Your prayer could sound something like, "God, I don't even know if I believe you're real, but if you are, will you please help me to believe in you?" I believe God delights in our honest attempts to seek him. He sent his only Son to die on the cross for your sins because he loves you more than you could ever know. As you decide to carve out time to draw closer to him, rest assured that he is going to draw closer to you, too.

These are some of the ways we can practically engage in spiritual warfare and this is how we begin to fight. As you leave your concentrated time with God, your interaction with him doesn't have to end for the day. Prayer isn't limited to what you write in a journal or restricted to the privacy of your home. Our days can be filled with ongoing communication with God. The reality is that he loves you and wants to speak to you.

As you go throughout your day, he is right there and wants relationship with you. Believing this truth can look like asking Him for strength as you walk into a challenging meeting or for wisdom and grace as you discuss finances with your spouse. It can also look like simply giving Him thanks for the moments you're carving out to read these pages. God's communication back to you may not sound like an audible voice from the sky, but God can communicate in a variety of ways. He may call to mind a scripture you recently read or you might feel a reassurance that He cares for you. Regardless, practicing more intentional time spent with God will continually refocus the lens of your heart on God's truth, and this is how we engage (and experience victory) in spiritual warfare. This is how we fight.

Cultivating a relationship with a God you can't see does not come naturally to anyone, so don't be discouraged in this process. Sometimes people have a tendency to expect speaking to and hearing from God to be as natural and fluid as riding a bike; this has not been my experience. That being said, God wants to be found by you and will be faithful to you along the way as you seek him with all your heart. A relationship with God is a lifelong pursuit and there is simply no way for me to do it justice in one chapter, but these suggestions can help you to get started and to begin to connect with God on a daily basis.

8
TAKING ANOTHER STEP

As the focus in your life begins to shift to what God desires for you, you'll notice that your thinking will begin to change. My hope is that you're already seeing where God is at work in your life and starting to think about how to pursue more of Him. Pursuing more of God is the catalyst that will propel you forward into the future you're hoping for, and it will breathe life into the practical steps you can take toward your vision, as well. Seeing your God-given vision become a reality starts by committing to your next step and by making small, but important changes.

If you're feeling overwhelmed with the vision you have, that's often a great indication that God is up to something. Recognizing you need God's help to turn your vision into a reality is a great place to be, even if it doesn't feel like it. It means your perspective is focused on things that are bigger than yourself. It means that this vision is big enough to inspire you, and that is exactly the motivation that will help you to plan out the next few steps.

After writing down your vision, you can begin to take some initial steps in the right direction. Those steps may simply look like reading a book on the topic that you desire to grow in, finding a group of people who share a similar passion, or changing a habit in your life. The most important thing is simply getting started. Sometimes the vision you have for your life isn't clear-cut and simple.

Before my wife and I had children, she worked in an office environment for several years. That was a time in her life where staying focused on vision was a challenge. Her primary tasks at work centered on balancing registers, reconciling accounts, and processing paperwork, but over time she began to see the vision that God had for that office. In the middle of daily mundane tasks, she and her co-workers would spend time talking about their lives, and day after day she found opportunities to share wisdom and shine light into the struggles her co-workers faced.

If the vision you feel God has given you is to have a significant impact for Christ in your workplace, an action step you might start with could be as simple as praying for your co-workers or boss every single day before walking in the door. And that could be just the beginning. You could sit down with other Christian businessmen or women and talk through what having an impact in the workplace could look like.

You could begin to study examples of people from the Bible like Daniel who made a difference in a culture that wasn't open to the message he wanted to share. Depending on your work environment, even choosing to read the Bible or another Christian book during your lunch break might spark the kind of conversation with those around you that you're hoping for. Those conversations might even open the door for a book study or Bible study after work. For others, maybe your action steps would be a little more indirect. Choosing a patient attitude when frustration is the easier choice can make a world of difference to those around you.

The more you think about how this could look for you personally, you'll begin to see there are probably several ways to impact those around you over the next few weeks, months, or year that will keep you focused on that vision. While having an impact in the workplace may not be a vision God has specifically placed on your heart, I hope you're beginning to see that whatever your vision is, there are always possible next steps.

Maybe the vision you feel planted in your heart is something huge, and it seems fairly specific. Rather than struggling with how to gain clarity, you might just feel overwhelmed at how to break the idea down into something you could actually do. Seeing a vision like that come to life requires thinking through specific steps, starting small, and building a strategy. Through the years of serving in a church that cares for the world and the community, I've seen people start with a vision like building schools and hospitals in Kenya, reforming the quality of foster care in our state, or reducing the crime level in our city, and then find ways to make it happen. These stories are inspiring, but they always start with a vision followed by some fairly unimpressive first steps.

Molly and George Greene started an organization called Water Mission International and their initial steps were relatively ordinary compared with the extraordinary impact their organization is now having. Their story is highlighted on the Water Mission website, watermission.org:

> *In 1998, our founders, Molly and George Greene, were operating an environmental engineering company in Charleston, South Carolina when they heard about the devastation in Honduras caused by Hurricane Mitch. After receiving a request for multiple water treatment systems in Honduras, and being unable to find existing systems that would work, George and his team of engineers took action to build such a system—and thus the idea for Water Missions International was born.*

Prior to their trip to Honduras, Molly and George hadn't been confronted with the reality that many people in the world do not have access to clean drinking water. After they came to this realization, they founded Water Mission to help solve a problem that many didn't even know existed. While the impact of their vision is truly extraordinary, the first step of their vision was simply meeting with a few engineers to see if they had any new ideas for a water treatment system that would work. The beginning steps of their vision were essentially no different than the steps you can take as you begin the journey toward your own.

Based on the vision you've written down, what are your next steps? Who could you meet with or what book could you read? Your vision may seem overwhelming, but God is bigger and greater than every obstacle we face. He will empower you and help you with each step along the path he's called you to take. Before you begin writing the specific steps you'll take next, I'd love for you to join me in this prayer:

> *God, as my friend prayerfully considers and takes to heart what he or she believes you're leading, I pray you would give wisdom and peace. I humbly ask that you would help them to see the specific and clear action steps you're calling them to take and give them everything they need to move closer to your vision for them. I thank you, Father, for their heart and desire to serve you and I pray you would bless them abundantly with your presence and power as they embark on this exciting journey. In Jesus' name I pray. Amen.*

9
EMBRACING THE JOURNEY

I really like getting things done. Actually, I really like getting to the finish line. No matter what the situation or task in front of me, the idea that it's about the journey and not the destination is not an easy pill for me to swallow. Because I'm picturing the sweetness of reaching that finish line from the second I begin, it's easy for me to overlook the importance of the simple processes of daily life. But going after the vision God has called us to is a lifelong pursuit.

We're not engaged in this journey for a plaque or a certificate and there is no "arrival" this side of heaven. To be sure, there are certainly incredible rewards along the journey, but the best rewards don't come with your name printed on them. Running after your vision is not about your accomplishments, but instead it's about the man or woman you're *becoming*.

Achieving an incredible goal without your character growing to look more like Christ is ultimately an empty pursuit. That may seem like a harsh truth, but achieving something always means sacrifice. God's vision for you is not to sacrifice your personal character on the altar of achievement. This idea of valuing who we are *becoming* above the goal often leads to a significant change in priorities. I would say God might just allow your life plans to be frustrated if that's ultimately what's best for your soul and your walk with him.

Placing your focus on the process of becoming instead of the arrival requires the perseverance of a marathon and not a sprint. When it comes to personal growth and progress towards every vision God gives you, celebrating the small victories that bring you a little closer each day will help you to stay encouraged. What can you do today or this week that will bring two percent growth in the right direction? A perspective like this can help you through times of discouragement and disappointment when they inevitably come. Making the process of personal growth and transformation your focus can develop your character in ways that will help you to continue pursuing your vision over the long haul.

Becoming the man or woman God is calling you to be takes precedence over whatever he is calling you to do or achieve. Before you meet a girl worth waiting for, God wants to make you a man worth waiting for. Before you start the business of your dreams, God wants to develop you into the leader that can steward that business. I'm not saying that God wants you to be perfect before you try anything, it's simply that God always seems to place the emphasis on the state of your heart over the condition of your circumstances. What I am saying is that we should be intensely focused on the men and women God's calling us to become. This is a process that requires grit and perseverance.

Currently, I'm a teacher, pastor, spoken word artist, and writer. I love using the gifts I've been given in these areas, but as soon as I make any one of them the target of my focus, I've begun to lose my way. A deeper relationship with God is what I'm pursuing. As I learn more and more to embrace the daily process of growth, I love that it's possible to lead and not have things figured out. I'm thankful he is molding and shaping me to become the person he had in mind when he created me, and I lead by inviting others to grow alongside me.

This is why we need to make sure we assess the journey towards our vision before we decide to embark on it. Most of the growth God wants to do in us happens behind closed doors. It happens when no one is watching and no one is applauding. I would even say that most of the growth God wants to develop in our lives happens between our own two ears, and every disappointment or discouragement will test the depth of our motivation. God will also provide a community around us along the path toward our vision, but our relationship with God is what will help us stand strong when no one else is standing with us. The only enduring reason to pursue a vision, plain and simple, is because God has called you on it. We never have complete certainty on this, but this is hopefully why we start pursuing the vision to begin with. We can know that God is the one who called us on the journey, and he's the one who will see us through to the other side. Holding a genuine belief that God has called you on this journey will help you persevere when the road inevitably becomes difficult.

10
LINKING ARMS

In this age of social media and constant digital interaction, it's not uncommon for people to live "connected" lives that lack true relationships. Having at least a couple of people who know the real you is a vital part of pursuing God's vision for your life. Who are the people in your life that know the real you? It's easy to make this kind of friend when you're young. Those friends, or that one friend, knew what you looked like when you cried and they were the ones you couldn't wait to share good news with. Friends like this are so valuable, but as we grow older, it can be easy to grow distant from them.

By the time we're adults, few people, if any, actually know the real us. We say we're "doing fine" in the pits and valleys of daily life, partially because we've forgotten what being transparent, let alone vulnerable, even feels like. Being transparent comes easily for me, but there's a difference between transparency and vulnerability. Transparency means sharing surface struggles in my life that don't require any real risk to share. Vulnerability means having the courage to share information and wounds in my life. It means confiding in someone, trusting they're going to love me regardless.

Transparency is important, but it doesn't build relationships by itself. Taking steps to make your heart vulnerable with a few, trustworthy people around you will deepen the friendships, and begin to build a network of support for when you hit the difficult days you're bound to experience as you pursue God's vision for your life.

I, like so many others, believed from an early age that I shouldn't need help from others in life. I thought that maturity meant being able to handle everything all on my own and that needing help was a weakness. As I grew and matured however, I began to see the foolishness of that perspective and how essential other people are in my journey. They are the precious people who love me even more for having the courage to bring my struggles into the light. They believe in me, know my heart, and understand that I'm a real human being with real struggles. Relationships that are characterized by vulnerability require time, patience, and trust to develop, but they're worth every bit of the effort it takes to forge them.

Walking in the vision God has for you will never happen alone. Friendships that are characterized by vulnerability are essential, but there are other necessary relationships that will guide you along the journey of your vision. Just as a family isn't made up of only brothers and sisters, there are other layers to the family of God. Cultivating relationships with some who are older and wiser than you will grow and stretch you. Some people may serve as a mentor in your life for a season and others for a lifetime, but that isn't the point. The point is to spend time with someone who is further down the road than you and who has gained wisdom by walking the path you're currently on.

In my ten plus years of pastoring, I have greatly benefited from a handful of older, wiser people who have been incredible mentors to me. The struggles you're facing aren't new; someone has walked them before, and someone else will face them after you. You have the opportunity now to learn and grow from others' wisdom. Try stepping out of your comfort zone and ask a wiser individual to get coffee with you on a regular basis. If you're a dad of young kids, sitting down with another dad whose kids are teenagers or already out of the house will expand your perspective of your own circumstances. If you spend some time thinking about those already in your life, there may already be someone coming to mind. Look for someone who has walked the same path ahead of you. It will take some vulnerability to seek out a mentor-type relationship, but most often that person will be grateful for the opportunity.

For me, one of those mentors is Pastor Jerry McSwain. Pastor Jerry and I have been meeting off and on for over twelve years. When I was in my early twenties, I asked Jerry if he'd be willing to sit down with me and it grew from there. Jerry and I don't see eye to eye on everything, but that's not the point. He has grown children, a mature marriage, and a solid walk with God. When I talk to Jerry, I sit in the role of student and honor him by listening to his experiences and perspective. While Jerry has graciously spent hours upon hours of time with me over the years, I consider it my responsibility to be the primary initiator in the relationship.

If Jerry and I haven't talked in a while, I make it my job to jump on the phone and call him. To learn something from someone else requires humbling yourself and submitting to their wisdom and experience. My hunch is that this is why many people don't have this kind of relationship in their life. 1 Peter 5:5 (NKJV) says that, "God resists the proud, but gives grace to the humble." To put it simply, you will not be able to achieve God's vision for your life if you resist the humble road.

There are also some seasons of your journey where friends and mentors can't provide the amount of guidance you need. In those times, a Christian counselor may be a tremendous help. You don't need to wait until you're at the end of your rope to find a counselor. If you recognize that you've been stuck in certain habits or behaviors that you struggle to move past on your own, a counselor can walk through those challenges with you. A good counselor is someone who sees him or herself as partnering with God for the ongoing restoration of your soul. You could have all the right relationships, the right skills and the right opportunities, but without the right perspective, you will be greatly hindered as you pursue God's vision for you. Counseling might not be needed for everyone, but the bottom line is simple: any vision worth pursuing is simply way too big to pursue alone.

If you haven't already done this, I encourage you to begin praying that God would show you who he has strategically placed around you to help shoulder your burden as you move forward in your journey. Keep in mind that God has probably already brought some others into your life so that you can help carry the load of their vision just as others can do the same for you. As followers of Christ, our individual pursuits are ultimately tied to a collective vision that looks like God's kingdom advancing on earth. This is how life is meant to be lived; in the context of community. Community is a powerful force to be reckoned with when it is taken as seriously as we see displayed in the Bible.

Acts 2:42-47 paints a picture that we can all aspire to. It's not simply a group book study or some kind of church program. While these examples can provide opportunities for community to grow, they're not enough on their own. Real community takes time and investment and much to our dismay, there's nothing formulaic about it. It's people who are strongly devoted to one another and who are committed to fighting alongside each other. You know you have a place at the table and that people love you for who you are. This is not something that's created by accident, but it is something we can pray for and seek out intentionally. Experiencing community and true relationships is innately tied to experiencing success as we pursue the vision God has for each of our lives.

11
ORDINARY EFFORTS, EXTRAORDINARY POWER

The thought of trusting God often feels daunting to me. I lost my mom to cancer when I was almost ten, and that experience affected me in many ways, as you can imagine. I didn't have guidance or Godly wisdom offered to me as I navigated the grief I experienced and there were several lies that really took root in my heart. I began to believe the lie that most people weren't trustworthy and that abandonment or rejection was almost inevitable. I began to believe that the world was a dark, lonely place, and I would always be better off on my own. After I encountered God in college and my life was changed dramatically, I started to realize that I had been harboring a belief that God would abandon me as well.

In my journey toward the vision God has given me, God has shown me over and over when I revert back to thinking he isn't trustworthy. I want to believe he's going to show up in my circumstances and move on my behalf, but when push comes to shove, it's easy to doubt that he actually will. It's strange that sometimes it feels safer to not put our trust in God at all simply because we fear disappointment. But God has shown me time and time again that he is incredibly faithful, and we *can* trust him with our whole heart and soul. We are not in this alone. As we bring our ordinary efforts to the table, God will step in with his extraordinary power and presence.

As you take steps to bring your vision to reality, you will grow and make progress toward that picture of your future. God sees those efforts, and he multiplies them.

One of the most precious things God offers us is his ongoing, loving presence. When we surrender our lives to Jesus Christ, the Holy Spirit comes to take residence in our hearts and he promises to never leave us or forsake us. (Hebrews 13:5 NIV) His presence is undeniable when we experience it, and God graciously reminds us of his faithfulness to us as we pursue his plans and purposes for our lives.

People often say, "God never gives us more than we can handle." I don't believe that for a second. On the contrary, I believe God never gives us more than *he* can handle, and when we're in over our heads, he's right there to show us he's been present all along.

Pastor Mark Batterson said, "Everyone wants a miracle but no one wants to be in an impossible situation that necessitates one." God sometimes lets us get into situations where we're in over our heads, so that our only option is to trust in him. It's not that he wants us to feel the pain of those circumstances, but he wants us to feel He doesn't do this to cause us pain, but rather because he loves us.

In addition to his presence, God will continue to lead you with his vision for your life with direction and guidance. God cares more about his will being done in our lives than we do. As simple as that may sound, sometimes it's easy to forget that. I've met with people before who are desperately trying to twist God's arm to get him to do his will in their lives. While I understand and relate to this sentiment, doesn't something seem backwards about it?

The only reason any of us even want God's will to begin with is because he has been pursuing us. God will always give timely direction as we pursue the visions he places on our hearts. Of course there will be times when you think you need an answer, and it doesn't come. That can easily lead to feelings of tension and frustration, but God is a faithful Father. He will provide what you need, when you need it.

Seeking God's direction is rooted in studying his Word and prayer. These disciplines are vital to the life of a follower of Jesus as they are direct channels for us to connect with God relationally. Seeking to hear from God through time alone with him in silence and solitude is also important in our fast-paced and crazy world.

Romans 12:1-2 (NIV) says, "Therefore, I urge you, brothers and sisters, in view of God's mercy, to offer your bodies as a living sacrifice, holy and pleasing to God—this is your true and proper worship. Do not conform to the pattern of this world, but be transformed by the renewing of your mind. Then you will be able to test and approve what God's will is—his good, pleasing and perfect will."

As we spend time in God's word and in his presence, he gradually transforms our minds, so that our thoughts and feelings eventually begin to mirror his thoughts and feelings. This process of transformation is how we become increasingly able to discern the mind and heart of God. As we do that, we are more able to walk in his will, and he will grant us his peace, joy and direction to see us through to the end.

One of the things we must understand about God is he is a supernatural Father. Isaiah 55:9 (NIV) says, "As the heavens are higher than the earth, so are my ways higher than your ways and my thoughts than your thoughts." As you set your mind and heart on following God and passionately pursuing the vision he puts on your heart, expect God to move on your behalf in unexpected ways. He works in different ways in the lives of different people, but one thing is for sure, he will show up for you. He is going to intervene in ways that are far beyond your ability to anticipate or predict. Think for a moment about the miracle in Matthew 14 where Jesus multiplied five loaves and two fish to feed a crowd of thousands.

As we pursue God's vision for our lives, he will repeatedly take our ordinary efforts and add his extraordinary power to them to achieve supernatural results. There are countless other examples throughout the pages of scripture that reveal God's desire to do this for his children, but I'm confident that he's doing it in your life too. The encounters we have with God's presence, direction, and transformative power are the most convincing reminders of God's intentions for you. If he has pursued you before, will he not do it again?

12

THROUGH A WIDER LENS

You have been invited by God himself into a life that is far greater than anything you could imagine on your own. As we move forward in our individual journeys, it's helpful for us to be reminded of those who have successfully fulfilled the visions that God gave them. One of those individuals is the apostle Paul. The New Testament is filled with words expressing the vision God gave him, and even a quick glance at his life would tell you he kept that vision in focus.

As Paul neared the end of his life and knew his time on earth was drawing to a close, he wrote a letter to his disciple, Timothy. In 2 Timothy 4:6-8 (NASB), Paul said, "For I am already being poured out as a drink offering, and the time of my departure has come. I have fought the good fight, I have finished the course, I have kept the faith; in the future there is laid up for me the crown of righteousness, which the Lord, the righteous Judge, will award to me on that day; and not only to me, but also to all who have loved His appearing." Paul did it! He knew he hadn't lived perfectly, but he fought long and hard to live out the life Christ had called him to. What an incredible feeling this must have been for a weathered man who had given everything he had.

Vision matters more than words can communicate. Because of the nature of the opposition we're up against, no one simply drifts in the right direction, the direction God has for us. As Zig Ziglar famously said, "If you aim at nothing, you will hit it every time." While aiming at nothing is certainly a tragic stance, it's equally tragic to aim our lives at a misguided vision. We can spend day after day, week after week, month after month and year after year pursuing goals that are not worthy of the life God has for us. Think of Paul's celebratory words as you recall the unfortunate story of the Olympic sharp-shooter, Matt Emmons. He spent year after year, month after month in preparation for those games, and missed the mark when it mattered most. Paul, on the other hand, focused everything he had on what truly matters, and the effects will reverberate throughout all eternity.

God has called us to so much more than anything we could ask for or imagine (Ephesians 3:20-21 NIV). God has an incredible plan for your life. He wants to use you more than you know for purposes that fit his extraordinary nature. His plans are, as Jeremiah says, "to prosper you and not to harm you, plans to give you hope and a future (Jeremiah 29:11 NIV)." To achieve that purpose, it must begin with a resolve to focus your life on God. As you surrender your heart to Jesus Christ as Lord and engage in a daily relationship with him, the focus of your life will gradually shift to God and others. As that begins to happen, you'll find yourself with a heart posture that allows you to receive the vision God has for you.

As I write this, I can't help but wonder how others around you will be impacted by the vision God has given you. Go back and read the vision you wrote down. One year from now, how would you like to feel when you read those words again? I encourage you to pray and submit them once again to God, inviting his power to change the course of your story.

Living with vision will keep you focused on what matters most and one day, like Paul, you too will be able to say that you fought the good fight and finished the race.

A FINAL THOUGHT

Proverbs 29:18 (NASB) says, "Where there is no vision, the people are unrestrained." The way I see it, we can look at the word "unrestrained" in two different ways. In this verse, it carries a negative connotation. In other translations it says, they "run wild" (NLT) or "perish" (KJV). I believe however, there's a different kind of unrestrained that God invites us to. When we're running in the path of God's commands, pursuing the direction he has for us, we'll experience a freedom we've never known before. Galatians 5:1 (NIV) says, "It is for freedom that Christ has set us free." God wants us to live in freedom, but it's a kind of freedom that many don't yet comprehend.

Our culture often defines freedom as being able to do whatever you want, whenever you want. While I understand the context of that definition of freedom, it is incomplete and inadequate. True freedom comes from walking in union with Christ in the plan and purpose he has for us. Submitting your life to someone else can seem limiting or confining at first glance, but this perspective misconstrues the character of God. Our lives are a gift from God given to us for purposes that are beyond our ability to comprehend. No matter what mistakes we've made, no matter how much we think we've blown it, there is still time for a comeback. We happen to serve a God who loves comeback stories.

Don't turn back, don't slow down, don't give up. By God's grace, you have what it takes to live out the vision God has for your life. There is only one you on this planet and no one but you can fulfill his purposes for you. No one else can be the father you can be to your children. No one else can be the daughter you can be to your parents. No one else has your distinct story or your unique gifts and abilities. God wants to weave them together to form a masterpiece that satisfies your soul and brings him glory. The time is now and the world is waiting for you to step into your God-ordained vision.

As I believe all important decisions begin, continue, and end in prayer, I invite you to pray this prayer along with me:

> *God, thank you for your faithfulness. Thank you for your love for me. I pray you would empower and equip me to fulfill the calling you've placed on my life. I recognize my life is not about me and that it is all about you. I repent for every part of me that has rebelled against and resisted your calling for my life. Thank you for what Jesus did for me on the cross. Thank you for his death and resurrection. I surrender my life to him, now and ask that you would use me however you want in this precious life you've given me. I submit to you my dreams, fears, and desires for the future. Use me however you want to, and I pray the glory of my life would be yours. In Jesus' name. Amen.*

ACKNOWLEDGEMENTS

Just as all God-given visions must be submitted to him, written down, fought for, planned carefully, and executed with patience and the support of others...so it has been with this book. To be an author was a vision that was planted in my heart several years ago, and it has only come to fruition in God's timing.

For Abbi, my amazing wife, thank you for inspiring, challenging, and supporting me. For my amazing sons, thank you for being constant reminders of God's faithfulness and for challenging me in each your own ways to be the father that God wants me to be.

For Pastor Greg Surratt, Pastor Josh Surratt, and the leadership at Seacoast Church, thank you for your continued belief and investment in me. I'm also ridiculously grateful for Terry Peterson for his tireless investment in this project. Thank you, my friend. While there are too many to individually list, I'm truly thankful for all my friends and church family. God continues to use your prayers and support for my family and I more than we ever could have dreamed possible.

I'm thankful for my dad, brothers and family in Connecticut. Simply put, I would not be who I am today if it weren't for you.

For everyone who reads this book, I wish you all the best as you pursue the vision God has for your life. As we choose to do that together, the world will be forever changed for the glory of God.

FROM THE AUTHOR

I gave my life to Christ when I was eighteen years old, and my life hasn't been the same since. Since the beginning of my journey in following Christ, I have had a consistent and growing passion for God's Word.

    I am passionate about sharing truth with others, and my favorite way to do that is through Spoken Word Poetry, Daily 1 Minute Messages, and as the pastor of Seacoast Church: West Ashley Campus in Charleston, South Carolina. The Lord blessed me with my wife, Abbi, and so much of what I have become is because of the strength God gave her. She loves fiercely and relentlessly and pushes me forward. We have three amazing sons, Isaac, Jonathan, and Samuel.

FIND MORE AT:

www.OfficialChrisRusso.com

facebook.com/officialchrisrusso

twitter.com/pastorrusso

instagram.com/pastorrusso

SHARE YOUR STORY & HEAR OTHERS:

facebook.com/1minutemessage

www.ingramcontent.com/pod-product-compliance
Lightning Source LLC
Chambersburg PA
CBHW031501040426
42444CB00007B/1172